NATIONAL GEOGRAPHIC

Ladders

TAMING THE WILD

The CHICKEN AND THE Egg

by Judy Elgin Jensen

Cock-a-doodle-do! Cock-a-doodle-do! It's early morning and time to get up! Today you'll search the forest edge for a few white eggs hidden away in a nest of leaf litter. At least that might have been your job 7,000 to 10,000 years ago if you lived in the jungles of southeast Asia. There, wild birds called red jungle fowl scratched the ground for seeds and insects. They laid eggs in the spring of the year. You might think they looked and sounded a lot like some chickens today, and there's a good reason for that.

Thousands of years ago, ancient people began to capture and raise some of the red jungle fowl. They liked the way the fowl looked. They liked the way the fowl tasted, too. So people eventually **domesticated** the fowl, or tamed, fed, and bred them as a source of food. That way the fowl would be nearby whenever they wanted to look at them, or to eat them or their eggs. Over time, because people kept only certain fowl, the features that people liked best improved. Eventually, some of the jungle fowl no longer looked much like jungle fowl. They looked more like the chickens you see today.

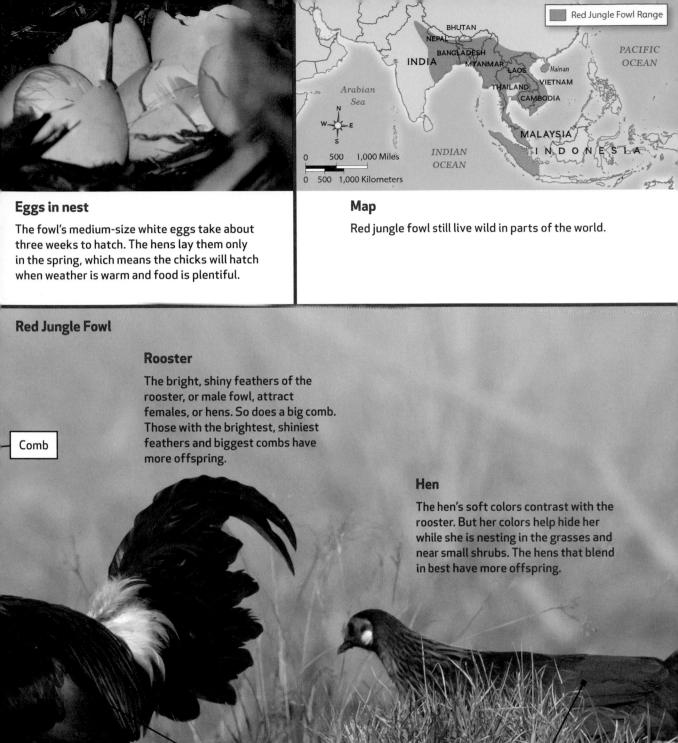

Eggs in nest

The fowl's medium-size white eggs take about three weeks to hatch. The hens lay them only in the spring, which means the chicks will hatch when weather is warm and food is plentiful.

Map

Red jungle fowl still live wild in parts of the world.

Red Jungle Fowl Range

Red Jungle Fowl

Rooster

The bright, shiny feathers of the rooster, or male fowl, attract females, or hens. So does a big comb. Those with the brightest, shiniest feathers and biggest combs have more offspring.

Comb

Hen

The hen's soft colors contrast with the rooster. But her colors help hide her while she is nesting in the grasses and near small shrubs. The hens that blend in best have more offspring.

Bright, shiny feathers

Feathers same color as grasses

Gray legs and feet

Chickens for Meat and Eggs

Today's domestic chickens differ from red jungle fowl because, over time, people preferred certain **traits**, or characteristics. As people raised the jungle fowl, they kept the ones that had fancier feathers, laid more eggs, or had tastier meat. This process of people choosing which individuals with preferred traits to mate is called **selective breeding**.

Through selective breeding, many different **breeds**, or kinds, of chickens resulted. Some breeds became important for producing meat and others for producing eggs. Farmers kept mating those with more meat or that laid more eggs, and eventually, other traits seemed to disappear. Today, large farms raise thousands of chickens that have almost identical traits. The chicken is the most common domesticated animal, with an estimated population of more than 24 billion.

White Cornish Rock

As people domesticated chickens, colorful feathers became less important to attracting a mate. Today, some chicken growers prefer all white-feathered chickens such as the white Cornish rock breed. When these chickens are processed and sold, bits of feathers that might remain aren't very noticeable.

Plymouth Rock

The amount of muscle, or meat, on a chicken such as the Plymouth rock, is a trait growers and eaters like. Through selective breeding, the amount of breast meat in certain breeds of chicken has doubled in just 30 years.

Rhode Island Red

Some chickens started laying eggs that were brownish, and people liked them. So they kept more of those chickens. Today, many shades of brown eggs exist, such as the eggs of the Rhode Island red. Some people think brown eggs are more nutritious, but that's not the case. All eggs are equal when it comes to nutrition.

Leghorn

People didn't want to wait until spring to eat eggs. They figured out that removing eggs from the nest would cause chickens to lay more eggs. Today, leghorns are just one kind of chicken that lays one egg every day or so, all year long. That is, if you keep taking the eggs away. If you don't, you might end up with baby chicks!

Heirloom Chickens

Over time, people have developed over 400 different breeds of chickens. Many people think a lot of the unusual breeds should be preserved. They think the breeds are valuable in the same way as family treasures, or heirlooms, are. People call these chickens heirloom breeds. Some look much like the red jungle fowl. Others? Well, see for yourself.

Derbyshire Redcap

This rose comb is just one way the comb grows. Other breeds have different shapes of combs or no comb at all.

Hamburgh Bantam

A bantam is a miniature chicken that weighs less than one kilogram (2.2 pounds).

Black Silkie

Underneath the silky black feathers is black skin and gray meat.

Blue Partridge Brahma

Foot feathers cover the legs and feet of these and some other kinds of chickens.

Gold Sebright

Most chickens are black, white, or red-gold. But this breed has more complicated feather colors and patterns.

Phoenix

The tail feathers of this breed can grow as long as 10 meters (30 feet).

Marans Chicken

Marans Egg
As the egg passes out of the body, a pigment, or color, is layered over the egg. The color can be scraped off when first laid.

Ameraucana Chicken

Ameraucana Egg
A blue pigment, or color, is made by this breed. When the hen produces an egg, the pigment combines with the other materials that make up the shell.

Selective breeding brings a vast array of food to our tables. But it also results in large numbers of individuals being almost identical. Hidden traits might exist in heirloom breeds that would help individuals resist heat or some harmful germ if the environment changes in the future. Keeping heirloom breeds helps ensure that a wide variety of traits continue to exist—just in case.

Check In What characteristics of red jungle fowl can you see in modern-day chickens?

From Wolf to Woof

by Judy Elgin Jensen

Cuddled up with a beagle or bounding along with a border collie, you might find it hard to believe that dogs are related to wolves. We call dogs "man's best friend" for their devotion to us. Wolves, on the other hand, seem a bit more, well, ferocious. Then why would ancient people bring wolves into their camps? Scientists are not sure they really did. Many scientists think that around 30,000 years ago, wolves started **domesticating** themselves by relying on people for food. How?

As stone-age people began to settle in groups, they left food scraps around their camps. Curious, and perhaps hungry, wolves crept ever closer for the food. Those individual wolves that were less fearful of people stayed close. Eventually the less-fearful wolves living close to people no longer mated with the "wild" wolves nearby. After many, many years, the two groups became completely separate.

Over thousands of years, the **traits,** or characteristics, of the tamer wolves began to change. The tamer wolves were smaller, grew wider skulls and shorter jaws, and had bigger litters of puppies. Their behaviors changed to ones that were friendlier to people. Eventually, they began to show forms of traits such as curly tails, floppy ears, and splotchy black-and-white coloring not present in wild wolves. Dogs were with us.

Dog ancestors were much like this gray wolf and her pup.

Around 8000 Years Ago

Deep in ancient central Africa, small curly-tailed dogs hunted alongside tribal people. They stayed somewhat separate from the people, yet depended on them, too. Silent hunters, the dogs wore "bells" made of nuts. That way the tribesmen could find the dogs and the prey they caught. The dogs rarely barked, but like wolves, they whined, growled, and chortled.

Eventually basenjis—their name today—were taken to Egypt where they became a favorite of Egyptian pharaohs. Carvings of their likenesses adorn the walls of the pharaohs' tombs. Some think the ancient Egyptian god known as Anpu or Anubis, protector of the dead, sports the head of a basenji.

The energetic basenji has changed very little over time. Even today, it doesn't seem to be fully domesticated when compared to other dogs. Basenjis' independent behaviors make them difficult to train. And, like wolves, they can only have puppies once per year. Other kinds of dogs can have at least two litters.

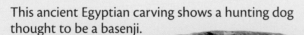
This ancient Egyptian carving shows a hunting dog thought to be a basenji.

Special Traits

🐾 Forehead is wrinkled when ears are perked up.

🐾 Tightly curled tail is turned up on the back.

🐾 Pointed ears can turn in several directions.

🐾 Hunts using both sight and smell.

Basenjis might be chestnut red, black, or a combination of the two colors in distinct patches or tawny brown with streaks of other colors. But all have white feet and chests, and a white tip on their curled tails.

Around 6000 Years Ago

Ancient Arabs used slim, fast-running dogs to help them hunt gazelles, which could run very fast too. Some individual dogs could dart after the twisting, turning gazelles and catch them. Many dogs immediately ate the gazelles they caught. Other dogs were a bit slower in catching gazelles, but they didn't eat them right away. That behavior was important because the people hunted gazelles for their own food.

So the ancient Arabs mated the fastest dogs with those that caught the gazelles but didn't eat them. And they chose which dogs mated over and over, which is **selective breeding.** The resulting dogs, called salukis today, run very fast and can twist and turn after darting prey with ease. Once they catch the prey, they just hold it and wait for their master to claim the prize.

Salukis had been taken to China by the year 600 A.D., where they were owned by emperors. One story says an emperor laid a mat in front of his saddle so the saluki could ride horses with him. Another emperor painted a picture of salukis. This painting stayed in the imperial collection for over 300 years.

The red seals show who owned or looked at the painting.

Special Traits

- 🐾 Slim rib cage and waist and very flexible backbone allows sharp twists and turns.
- 🐾 Steps can be 4 meters (12 feet) long when running.
- 🐾 Gallops at 65 kilometers per hour (40 miles per hour).
- 🐾 Hunts using keen eyesight.

Salukis today might have "feathers," or long hairs on the legs, and smooth coats. Their colors include white, cream, fawn, golden, or red, or a combination of black, tan, and white. They might also be grizzle and tan, which is a coloring similar to wolves. Grizzle is a banded pattern and each hair can have several colors. This coloring is similar to that of wolves.

Around 3000 Years Ago

Imagine living in Tibet, tucked high up by the Himalaya. Here the year-round bright sun never makes the air hot, even in summer. Ancient Tibetans herded yak and sheep. Their small, sturdy dogs, called apsos, acted as an alarm system in their tent homes—barking at intruders.

Early Tibetans might have chosen certain apsos to mate. But nature likely helped the selective breeding process as well. Individual apsos with double coats—one type of thicker fur close to the body and a longer, straighter layer of fur on top—would be warmer than some others. Those dogs with shorter legs stayed warmer too. Warmer dogs would more likely survive and have puppies. The puppies would have the same traits.

Tibet is also home to the Buddhist religion and the little dogs served the monks there. The loyal apsos, with their keen sense of hearing, alerted the monks to intruders. The monks also liked how the dogs looked like tiny lions because the lion is a sacred symbol to Buddhists.

This painting shows the Buddhist guardian of the north riding a lion. Apsos and some other breeds of dog have been called "lion dogs."

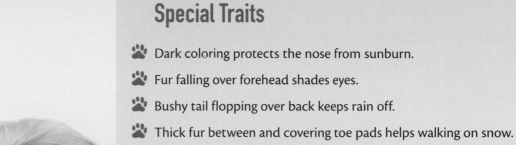

Special Traits

🐾 Dark coloring protects the nose from sunburn.

🐾 Fur falling over forehead shades eyes.

🐾 Bushy tail flopping over back keeps rain off.

🐾 Thick fur between and covering toe pads helps walking on snow.

🐾 Long hair and ears set high and held close keeps dogs warm.

Once apsos arrived in other countries, they were called Lhasa apsos, after the city of Lhasa in Tibet. Lhasa apsos today have an even longer, silkier outer coat because, over the last 100 years or so, people grew to like that trait. The shape of the forehead, length of the snout, and shape of the jaw also differs from the original Tibetan apsos because of selective breeding.

Dogs Today

Selective breeding over time has resulted in the amazing variety of dogs seen today. In the past, people selected certain traits in dogs that made the **breed** better suited for work tasks. Some of those tasks required the dogs to be fierce and aggressive. More recently, people have selected for traits to change those behaviors because they no longer need the dogs to be aggressive.

Boxer

This breed was developed to run down and hold large game, such as bison. Its name comes from the trait of standing on its back legs and "boxing" with its front paws.

Shar Pei

Originally a Chinese farm dog, the breed's name means "sandy coat" because of its prickly feel. Ancient Chinese thought the wrinkles and its blue-black tongue could scare away evil spirits.

Bull Terrier

In the late 1800s, a dog dealer began mating bulldogs with a breed of white terrier that no longer exists. Originally they were fighting dogs, but today they are described as clownish and playful.

Bloodhound

Over 1000 years old, the breed's name refers to efforts to keep the bloodline pure. Its sense of smell is so keen that evidence discovered by a bloodhound can be used in a court of law.

Bulldog

This breed was developed to anger and attack bulls. When the tradition died out, people liked the dog's looks so they selected for behavior traits. Today, the breed's nature is agreeable and lovable.

Dalmatian

The only spotted breed, its reputation as a firehouse dog goes back to horse-drawn fire trucks. The dogs had a calming effect on the horses and they protected the equipment.

Belgian Sheepdog

This breed was developed around 125 years ago. During World War I, many served as message carriers and some pulled machine guns. Today, many work as search and rescue dogs.

Chinese Crested

This breed can be either mostly hairless or powderpuff—with long hair all over—even in the same litter of puppies. In the 1200s, the dogs sailed on Chinese ships to kill rats.

Brussels Griffon

Originally this breed lived in stables to catch rats, but people liked their nature and soon brought them inside. They are the bearded dogs described in some old Belgian folk tales.

Great Dane

Among the tallest of breeds, its original job was to hunt wild boar. Later, people selected for behaviors that resulted in a human companion and guard dog that usually lives inside.

Chihuahua

A tiny breed, some think it was developed from a Mexican dog that was mated with a hairless dog brought by explorers—perhaps the Chinese crested.

Boxerdoodle . . . Dalmadoodle . . . Doodleman Pinscher . . . Schnoodle . . . Shepadoodle . . .

What do all these "doodle" dogs have in common? That's right—poodles! Most dogs shed, or lose hairs, daily. But poodles have a curly single coat that reduces the effects of shedding. The curly texture of their hair traps those falling out. So the breed is a favorite for mating with other breeds. The puppies have traits of both parents, such as a poodle's coat and a dalmatian's spots. Through selective breeding, people continue to develop dogs with the specific traits they want.

Poodle + **Labrador** = **Labradoodle**

Poodles respond well to obedience commands.

Labrador retrievers are athletic and good-natured.

Labradoodles were first bred for use as guide dogs for the blind. They are trained easily and are less likely to cause allergic reactions.

Many people, however, think the best breed of dog is one that is no specific breed at all. Called mutts or mongrels, no one set of traits describes what they look or act like. They might have the snout of one breed, ears of another, fur of another, build of yet another, and nature of yet another! When two mutts mate, you never really know what traits will actually show up in the puppies. They could look entirely different from the parents, or almost exactly like one or the other.

Over at least 30,000 years of nature and people selecting which individuals would mate with which led these animals from wolf to woof. Because of those selections, dogs show the greatest variations of any one kind of animal on Earth. And we love it.

Check In   How does selective breeding affect the traits of offspring?

Veggies: BIGGER and BETTER

by Julia Osborne

More than 6,000 years ago, people living in what is now Mexico began to **domesticate** a wild grass called teosinte (tay-o-SIN-tee). Why should you care? Because they domesticated this grass, you get to bite into a luscious ear of corn, snack on popcorn, and eat tortillas.

Over time, farmers collected seed kernels from wild teosinte plants with the most desirable **traits,** or characteristics. Perhaps the plants had more kernels on their small cobs or kernels that were a little plumper and easier to grind. When they planted those kernels, the plants that grew had more of the desirable traits too. Over many generations, their crops became less and less like the wild teosinte plants. Farmers had transformed teosinte into corn.

Teosinte

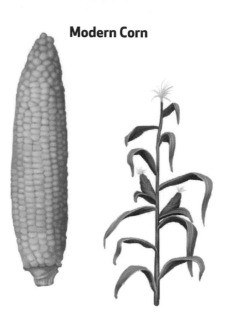

Modern Corn

- Branching and grasslike
- Kernels covered by a hard shell
- Small cobs
- Few, 5 to 12, kernels on cob

- A single, tall stalk
- Kernels without a shell
- Large cobs
- Up to 500 kernels on a cob

By 4,500 years ago, corn was being grown in many parts of North America, South America, and the Caribbean. When Columbus arrived, "Indian corn" was taken back to Europe. Today corn is a major source of food for people and livestock around the world. Farmers have used **selective breeding,** or the choosing of which individuals to mate, to develop many different kinds of corn. They have also increased the number of corn kernels that each plant produces.

∨ Kernels that contain lots of water pop open when heated.

∨ The glassy, rainbow colors of these kernels look like gem stones.

Russet Burbank

Shapely Potatoes

Each year, the average person in the United States eats about the same amount of potatoes—baked, mashed, and fried—as two fourth-graders weigh! Most of those potatoes are brown, red, or gold. But if you lived in Peru or Bolivia in South America, you would see potatoes of many shapes and shades of brown, blue, purple, and red.

People living in the Andes Mountains domesticated wild potatoes at least 7,000 years ago. About 450 years ago, Spanish explorers took potatoes to Europe. From there, potatoes were moved to other parts of the world. Potato plants grow best in places such as Ireland, Germany, Russia, and northern China, where the weather is cool and wet. In the United States, they grow especially well in northern states such as Idaho and Maine.

Today, farmers grow many different **strains** of potatoes. A strain is like a **breed,** but refers to plants instead of animals. Something to keep in mind is that even though potatoes grow underground, they are not roots. Instead, they are fleshy, underground stems.

Potatoes of Peru and Bolivia

Fig

Blue

Whip Made of Dry Animal Skin

Black Sweet

Puma's Paw

Feet of the Lequecho Bird

Black-and-White Spiral

Makes the Daughter-in-Law Cry

High Mountain Village

Ashes of the Soul

Woven Vest

Pork Dish

Strong Morning Frost

High Altitude Flower

Yellow Flower

Designer Kale

All of these plants aren't just vegetables, they're actually the *same* **species,** or kind of plant. Scientists call the plant *Brassica oleracea.* The species *Brassica oleracea* is a mustard plant that grows wild around the Mediterranean Sea. Its thick, dark leaves were a favorite food of the ancient Greeks and Romans. The leaves they ate were very similar to the thick, crinkled leaves of modern kale. If you live in the southern United States, you've probably eaten a closely-related form called collard greens.

Since Roman times, farmers have continued to use selective breeding to modify the original mustard plant. Focus on different plant structures resulted in some amazingly different forms of *Brassica oleracea.*

Farmers selected leafy forms of the parent *Brassica oleracea* to produce modern-day kale.

Forms of *Brassica oleracea*

Broccoli
Farmers selected parent plants with thick stems and lots of flower buds.

Brussels sprouts
Farmers selected parent plants that had tight clusters of leaves growing up the stalk. These leaf clusters formed tiny heads.

Cauliflower
Farmers selected parent plants with tight bunches of flowers.

Cabbage
Farmers selected parent plants with very short stems, which caused the leaves to grow close together. Eventually their selective breeding produced a plant with leaves that formed a tight ball or head.

Kohlrabi
Farmers selected parent plants with fleshy stems at the base of the plant.

Succulent Squash

Pumpkins and squash originated with Native Americans before Columbus took these foods back to Europe, where they soon became popular sources of food. As a result of selective breeding, squashes today come in an enormous variety of shapes and sizes. Summer squashes, such as zucchini, have soft skins and must be eaten soon after they are picked. Winter squashes have hard skins, so they can be stored for several months.

Forms of winter squashes include butternut, calabaza, crookneck, Hubbard, kabocha, spaghetti, and turban. The largest squashes are pumpkins. In fact, pumpkins are the biggest vegetables in the world. And they are also the biggest fruits, technically speaking, because they have seeds. Some people compete to see who can grow the most enormous pumpkins.

Butternut Squash
The butternut squash's sweet, nutty flavor resembles pumpkin.

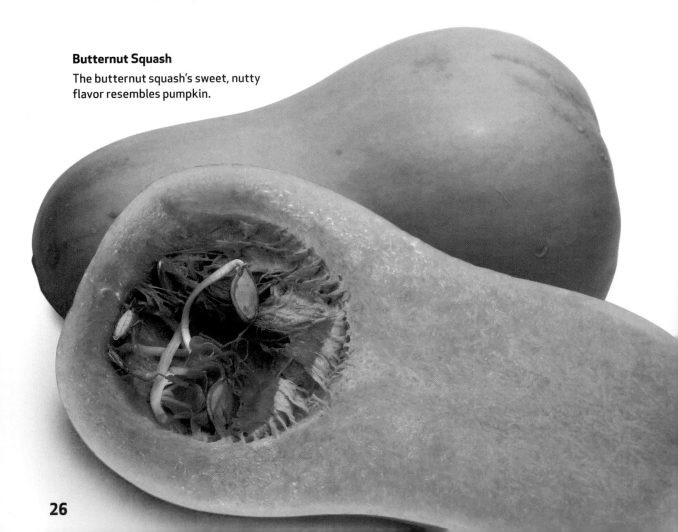

Kinds of Squash

Crookneck Squash
The bumpy skin and bent neck sets the crookneck squash apart from other squashes.

Turban
Turned upside down, the squash gives the appearance of a turban atop a person's head.

Pumpkin
Not only do people eat pumpkin flesh, they eat pumpkin seeds and pumpkin flowers.

Spaghetti Squash
When cooked, the flesh of the spaghetti squash form strings that look like spaghetti.

Acorn Squash
Most acorn squashes are dark green, but some are golden yellow or even all white.

Hubbard Squash
The skin of the hubbard ranges from green to light grayish-blue, and the squashes can be quite large.

Suppose you wanted to use a selective breeding process to create a new kind of vegetable. What would you start with? What traits would you focus on? What would it look like?

Check In How does selective breeding affect fruits and vegetables?

Saving Seeds
by Judy Elgin Jensen

The **domestication** of plants has a good side and one that is, well, perhaps not so good. Through **selective breeding,** new and improved crops give us more food. Corn plants produce more seeds for breads, sweeteners, and cereals. Tomatoes that are all about the same size are easier to pack and ship to distant stores. People like apples that stay crispy longer, even if they might not taste as sweet as other apples. And it's easier to build a machine to harvest soybean plants if all of the plants are about the same size. When these new **strains,** or **breeds,** are developed, most farmers grow them instead of the older strains. Yet many people worry about how domestication creates huge numbers of plants that are identical in almost every way.

What if something happens in the environment, such as a new disease? Or what if weather patterns shift, making a region a little warmer and drier? Almost all the plants of one kind could die off. So many people want to preserve heirloom strains, or older ones that show a lot of differences from plant to plant. Why do people have to make such an effort? Often the heirloom strains are forgotten until no one grows them any more. Therefore, the **traits,** or characteristics, needed to solve some future environmental problem might not be available.

To save the heirloom strains, people first had to figure out how to save their seeds. Each seed can grow into a plant with specific traits. Scientists and engineers designed seed vaults to protect and preserve the seeds. A seed vault is a huge, temperature-controlled warehouse where seeds can be safely stored. Seed vaults allow people to preserve millions of seeds for hundreds of years. One of the most famous is the state-of-the-art Svalbard Global Seed Vault in Norway. It can save over four million seeds. Let's visit to see how it is designed.

Dr. Cary Fowler studies the importance of differences in plant traits. Here, he holds two containers of heirloom pea seeds. The entrance to the seed vault is in the background.

Inside a Seed Vault

To visit the Svalbard Global Seed Vault, you fly to an island in the Arctic Ocean. There, the vault is located underground. Inside the air is cold—minus 18°C (minus 0.4°F)! Even though the temperature is below freezing, the seeds don't die. Instead, the seeds are in a dormant, or waiting, stage. Seeds can remain in this dormant stage for many, many years—even hundreds!

The vault is in a layer of ground that is always frozen. That way the inside of the vault will stay very cold even if the power goes out.

130m (425 ft.)

People keep an eye on the opening from a nearby airport. The entrance is kept lit during the dark winter months.

The rock in this area breaks easily. A steel sleeve protects the tunnel from the cracking rock.

Entrance

The lighting designed into the entrance won an award for its beauty.

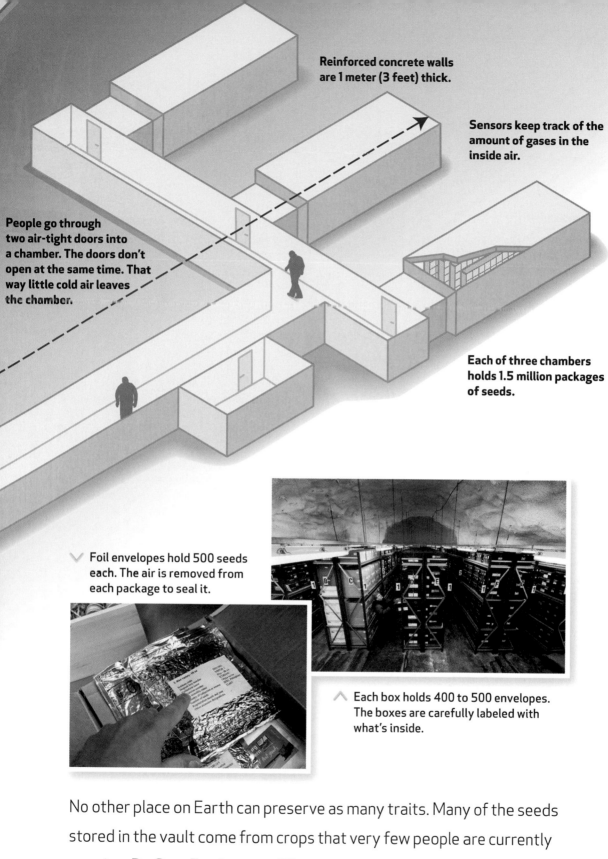

Reinforced concrete walls are 1 meter (3 feet) thick.

Sensors keep track of the amount of gases in the inside air.

People go through two air-tight doors into a chamber. The doors don't open at the same time. That way little cold air leaves the chamber.

Each of three chambers holds 1.5 million packages of seeds.

Foil envelopes hold 500 seeds each. The air is removed from each package to seal it.

Each box holds 400 to 500 envelopes. The boxes are carefully labeled with what's inside.

No other place on Earth can preserve as many traits. Many of the seeds stored in the vault come from crops that very few people are currently growing. Dr. Cary Fowler says, "This is an insurance policy for the world's most valuable natural resource."

Check In How and why do people save seeds for long periods of time?

Discuss

1. What do you think connects the four pieces in this book? What makes you think that?

2. How are red jungle fowl and chickens similar? How are they different?

3. Use examples from "The Chicken and the Egg," "From Wolf to Woof," and "Veggies: Bigger and Better" that show how selective breeding changed traits in living things.

4. What problem were engineers trying to solve in "Saving Seeds"?

5. Was the seed vault a good solution? Explain why or why not.

6. What do you still wonder about selective breeding and how living things change? What would be some good ways to find out more information?